Spike Press

Stan the Thug

Sally McKeown
Illustrated by Doug Hatfield

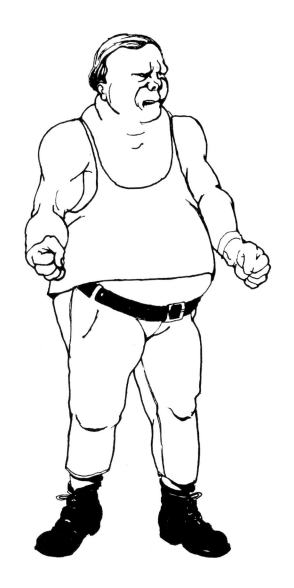

Stan was a thug.
He liked hitting people.

He pushed a man in a pub.
"I'll get you!" said the man.

Stan got him first.
Stan got 2 months.

Stan hit a man at a football match.
The man hit back.

There was a big fight.
Stan got 3 months.

When he got out, he kept out of fights.
He got a job.

Then one day he hit a man at work.
The man was the boss.
Stan got the sack.

Carol was Stan's wife.
She was fed up.
"Stop hitting people," she said.
"Next time you do it I'm off."

Stan went to look for a job.
He works as Big Al's minder.